Grip It: A Life Lived All-In

By R. A. Zoppo

For anyone who shelved their spark and wants it back.

Cover and interior design by R. A. Zoppo

First edition

ISBN: 979-8-9988501-3-4

For my children –
Who will one day face hard things.
I hope this helps you stand back up.

For my wife –
Who bet early, stayed steady, and saw the man before anyone else.

For my family —
Who handed me tools I didn't always understand, but use every day.

Author's Note

At the time of publication, most of the stories in this book are more than fifteen years old. Some I wrote almost twenty years ago. None of them were meant to become a book. I wrote them because some memories are too hot to carry inside — I needed them out of my body and onto the page.

I wrote to capture, but also to reflect. Writing gave me a way to distill and dissect events, to appraise my actions, and to keep growing. These dispatches became a mirror. And eventually, a kind of map. Not a map to follow — but one that might help you recognize a place in yourself.

These are short stories — dispatches from different seasons of a life. If one doesn't resonate, skip ahead.
Take what you need. Leave the rest.
The hardest-earned truths — the ones that go deepest — show up near the end. That's not by accident. The early stories are how I got there. They build the spine for what follows.

Names have been changed in a few places for privacy. But the emotions, the missteps, and the moments that matter — those are all real.

Thanks for meeting me here.
—R. A. Zoppo

I was here. I felt it all. I wrote this to preserve my fire.

Table of Contents

Prologue

If you saw me on the street, you'd never look twice.
I'm no Navy SEAL. Didn't go to an elite college. Certainly, never intended to write a book.

Most days I'm in the same sweatpants as yesterday and a T-shirt that's lost its fight with the dryer. No fancy car. I'm in my forties, living with my parents.
With my wife. And our three kids.

We're all huddled under one roof, eating grandma's spaghetti, while I chase a dream: trying to build a real estate project with my dad.
And no — the project isn't a new house for us.

So maybe this book should really be about my wife.
Because who but a superhero would agree to move in with the in-laws for a couple of years and hang on through two years of zero income?

She's a star.
She likes to say our ten beautiful years of marriage have felt like five minutes — underwater.

We're total opposites.
She was valedictorian.

I was in special ed, small groups, what you'd politely call "alternative classrooms."
And no, I didn't ride the short bus.
I rode my bike. But you get the idea.

This book is for you — from a guy who might be a little like you.

When I was twelve, my dad said something that stuck:

"You should think about things—Socrates said the unexamined life isn't worth living."

He didn't say it with a big speech. Just passing by. But something in me held on.
And over the years — between the setbacks, the hard knocks, the left turns — that line became a kind of compass.
Not because I live some perfect, examined life, but because I keep asking questions, even when the answers don't come easy.

Here's something my mom taught me through her tireless compassion:

Every permutation of the human experience is already in our DNA.
The hero. The coward. The addict. The warrior. The cynic. The poet.
We're not above each other — we're cut from the same old, worn-out cloth.

That truth can scare you. Or it can free you.

Because once you understand that all of it lives in you — the pain, the grace, the potential —
You stop looking down on yourself.

You stop looking down on people.
You start looking **across**.

You move through the world with a little more compassion,
both outward and inward.
You recognize that even the parts of you that feel lost or small
or tired — they're not defects.
They're the marrow of life — the raw material of being
human.

So, this book? It's for anyone who's shelved their spark.
For anyone who thinks they've lost it, or worse — convinced
themselves it was never there.
It is. It always was.
It's woven into the fabric of your DNA.

Let's coax that fire back to life.

Thanks for giving me your time.
And as the famous poem goes — *may the road rise to meet you.*

Part I – Edge & Ascent

Finding the edge. Facing yourself. Beginning without guarantees.

High Work

I had no business being up there. But I wasn't coming down.
—High Work

My palms were sweating through leather gloves, and the shingles beneath my sneakers felt like sandpaper over glass. I was standing at the edge of a three-story Victorian, roof pitch steep enough to make your calves scream and your brain whisper things like "what the fuck did I get myself into?"

That was day one.

I'd taken a job roofing during college — not because I knew anything about it, but because I'd always wanted a challenge. I was afraid of heights as a kid, so I figured I'd go straight at it. Roofing crews get paid more for steep roofs. The guy I worked for must've been allergic to flat ground. Every house we touched felt like the high dive at a pool where no one taught you how to swim.

There was one low roof we did that summer. It was like a day at the beach. I remember thinking, "Is this what normal people feel like at work?"

But that wasn't most days. Most days were brutal. Every time I climbed the ladder, I was expected to carry a bundle of shingles and a roll — no excuses. My back ached. My forearms burned. And still, my hands would sweat the moment I reached the ridge and looked down.

The thing no one tells you about fear of heights is: you don't get over it.
You just learn how to keep moving through it.
Your hands still sweat. Your knees still wobble.
You just stop expecting fear to leave. You learn how to carry it.

I was no hero up there. I was just a kid doing his job.
But eventually, I did it well. I learned how to move, how to keep balance, how to trust the soles of my sneakers and the work under my hands. Near the end of the summer, one guy said, "when you first got here, you climbed the ladder like a little bitch. Now? You know how to work."
And that — for me — was enough.

I think about that job more than people would guess.

It taught me how to respect fear, how to work tired, and how to shut up and carry something heavy when nobody's clapping for you.

But more than that, it taught me something bigger:

That every time I looked down from that roof, I wasn't just facing my fear. I was standing on the shoulders of every soul in my bloodline who had ever faced theirs — or run from it.

There are thousands of people behind each of us.
Our lineage is full of contradictions: killers, cowards, heroes, lovers, drunks, saints, workers, kings, addicts, fighters, servants, ghosts.

That's not just true for me.
It's true for you.

Whatever you've seen in others — whatever you've judged — it's in you, too. Maybe buried. Maybe close to the surface. But it's in the code.

And that truth? It's not depressing.
It's liberating.
Because it means you don't have to posture or pretend. You don't have to shrink from someone else's pain or puff up your own.

It means you can look across, not down.

That's what this book is about.

Not just the stories of roofs and broken backs and radioactive scans — but the invitation:
To remember what's already inside you.
To grip the thing you fear.
And to keep your footing, even when the ground tilts steep and high.

In the Ring Alone

I didn't win. But I didn't quit. That was the win.
—In the Ring Alone

I moved to Mexico while working for a company that managed event spaces—arenas, stadiums, and convention centers. To stay in shape, I joined a local boxing gym just a few blocks from my house. Learning to box in Mexico felt like learning to play hockey in Canada—it was the real thing.

My trainer, Alfonso, had coached with the Mexican Olympic team and still carried the fire. After my trial session, he accepted me as a student and took me under his wing.

For months, it was all drills. Endless repetitions, like *The Karate Kid* waxing cars. Some light sparring, but mostly technical work. I loved it, but I was itching for action. Training wasn't enough—I needed to test myself.

Then came the invitation: I'd been offered a slot in the local Golden Gloves tournament, just three weeks away. I crammed what I could between long hours at a demanding job— in a second language. But we hit a problem. Most Mexican boxers aren't 6 feet tall and 195 pounds. I needed a sparring partner—someone big.

Word went out to the gym and into the community.

Around that time, cartel violence in border states was escalating fast. Murders were nightly. Military convoys with mounted .50-caliber guns cruised city streets. Kidnappings had become common. Life was unraveling for anyone near that world.

Then, during a workout, word came down: someone would be at the gym the next night at 7 p.m. to spar.

As we joked in the steamy night air, a few cars pulled up near the gym — one of them a brand-new, top-of-the-line Mercedes. I remember that part clearly. Out stepped three guys in black leather jackets, stone-faced and silent. The vibe shifted instantly. Everyone got quiet.

That's when I understood why my coach hadn't shown up. He knew.

There were only a couple of us there that night, and suddenly, the gym felt different. Thinner. Heavier.

Someone said, "Don't make him mad."
Not advice— a survival tip.
Those kids knew. We all did. And we all carried it.

About to walk through our gym's door were guys who didn't need to speak to make their reputation known.

One of them—my sparring partner—was huge. Maybe 6'4", strong but not cut. He looked like an NFL lineman: not built for looks, but capable of moving a car.

Later, I wondered if Alfonso knew what was coming. That night—*the only night*—he didn't show up. In his place was a pro fighter from our gym, prepping for a bout in Las Vegas.

The stand-in told me to warm up. The big man changed in silence. I kept it friendly, shook hands. He acknowledged it, sort of.

Then we got in the ring.

No referee. No coaches. Just a brawl.

My trainer warned me: "Take it easy. Don't make him mad."

I ignored him. I wasn't going to throw soft punches to keep someone like this happy. I was going to take what I could. That was my mistake.

People underestimate punching. It's not muscle. It's timing, precision, alignment. When it all clicks—momentum, mechanics, bone on bone— it's devastating. I'd been refining that for years. I wasn't a great boxer, but I could *hit*.

And so, we fought.

The gym crowd hugged the ropes, flinching with every swing. The guy's crew stayed back, clad in black leather, only half-interested. None of that mattered. When someone tries to punch your face in, the world shrinks to one square ring.

He wasn't in great shape, though, and gassed quickly. He got frustrated that I could absorb his shots and keep moving. And he didn't like my power. He started to hold back, cautious.

It wasn't a clean match. It was a sweaty, awkward war. Bursts of violence between long silences. He grew more desperate, throwing flurries to end it, but I held my ground and returned fire.

We went for nearly an hour—exhausted, nauseous, and bruised.

He quit.

We were both sore. But he quit. I didn't. That part? That's always a choice.

Guantes de Oro

The whole arena screamed 'kill the gringo.' And still, I stepped forward.
—Golden Gloves

I thought I'd already stood alone in the ring. But that was just the warm-up

What happened before stayed with me. But the real test came next—the tournament.

The Golden Gloves tournament wasn't life or death—it was worse. It was sanctioned. It was public. And it was against someone who actually knew how to box.

[Mid-2000s, Mexico.]

They say your first real fight tells you everything you need to know.

Mine was in a secondary city of a million people in Mexico, under the lights of *Guantes de Oro* — Mexico's version of the Golden Gloves. It was my first tournament. My first official match. And I was ready.

I'd trained hard— beach runs, nose bleeds, aching hands. I was dialed in. Focused. And guys at my gym believed in me — believed that if I could land clean, I might be able to knock out my opponent.

Because — all humility aside — I hit like thunder.

But— I didn't just draw a good fighter. I drew **the** guy.
The former national amateur champion of Mexico.
And if you know boxing, that's no small thing.
It's like playing hockey against Canada's best.
You're not just up against a guy — you're stepping into the ring with a whole tradition.

I found out either at weigh-in or the day before. I don't remember exactly — just that it landed like a cold splash across the face. And by then, there was no backing out.

The arena was packed. Loud. His place. Not mine. The whole place felt like it belonged to someone else. As I stood under the lights, bouncing on soft canvas and trying to calm my breath, the crowd was already shouting:

"¡Mata el gringo!"
Kill the gringo.
It wasn't just hostile— it was ancestral.

You don't forget that. You don't pretend it didn't get in your head a little.

The bell rang and I came out hot — heavy hands, good stance, solid timing. I even thundered him a couple times. Clean shots. Ones that made the crowd go quiet for half a second. But it didn't matter. I couldn't close the distance. I couldn't break him. After two minutes on that soft mat, my legs were gone. My lungs were toast.

He out-boxed me — clean, smart, technical.
I lost by technical knockout.

And still — it felt like a win.

No one was in my corner except my trainer and the guy who lent me his trunks. That's it.
Even my girlfriend — Mexican — sat with my boss and coworkers on the *other* side of the arena. Later, they told me they started sweating the moment the bell rang.

And I loved it.

Afterward, we went out — my girlfriend, a big group of friends, and I — and grabbed food like it was any other night. I had a black eye, a full heart, and the sense that I'd done something real.

Because I didn't fight a nobody. I didn't get spoon-fed an easy matchup.
I boxed the best. In his country. In front of his people.
And I stood there.

That's what boxing gave me.
Not just pain and bruises — but *a proof of self*.
You don't have to win the fight to come out a fighter.

I lost. But I got up— every time.
And I felt like I'd won something bigger:
My place in the ring.
My place in myself.

Part II – Fire & Freefall

Adrenaline, chaos, danger, and the quiet lessons of unraveling.

The Deep Breath

Nobody knew what had just happened. So, I didn't say anything. I just kept walking.
—Deep Breath

My buddy Ed had lived in Guatemala for almost four years by the time I went to visit him. He actually came to visit me first, in rural El Salvador, before I ever saw his turf — and before the cave nearly swallowed me.

He rolled up to my place speaking Spanish slang that immediately earned him street cred with the kids sitting on the stoop kitty-corner from my digs. We spent a few minutes chatting with Doña Mati, my seventy-year-old landlord, before jumping on the bus headed for the coast. It was Christmas Eve, and we were ready to party. Her parting words were the same as always: "¡Pórtese bien!" – *Behave yourself!* I grinned and shot back, "¡Más todavía?"—*Even more than I already am?*

Weeks earlier, I had tried to book a reservation at the beach hostel, thinking it would be packed. My Salvadoran roommate, Samuel, had called a couple of times on my behalf — and was told it was full.

But when I called back myself, thick gringo accent and butchered Spanish on full display, we were magically confirmed.

Fucking jerks. Clearly discriminating against their fellow Salvadorans.

Had I been thinking, I would have switched hostels. But there was only one on El Tunco— a black sand beach pounded by Pacific waves and off the beaten path, so that would have meant switching beaches entirely. Still, I would have been proud to do it.

When Ed and I arrived, it was clear we were the only guests. The workers handed us the keys and told us to bang on a door down the street if we needed anything.

In Latin America, Christmas Eve is the night to celebrate with family. That meant every restaurant and store was closed. We would have gone hungry if not for the kindness of a family having dinner outside their house on the sandy road. The woman saw us sitting listless on the hostel stoop and asked if we'd eaten. When we said no, she brought us two huge plates overflowing with eggs, beans, and a stack of tortillas. It changed everything. Our moods flipped, and after dinner we watched fireworks burst through the suburban sky.

Ed had been itching to go caving in Guatemala. So, we signed up for a tour with a local guide and a small group, and made our way into the jungle.

With candles lit and water knee-deep, we stepped into the cave. The mouth quickly disappeared behind us and the light faded fast. The trek was only a few kilometers, and all twelve of us tourists pushed deeper into the darkness with nervous excitement.

The guide had a flashlight but preferred candles. Said they were a better way to tell time. When your candle was halfway done, you turned back. I wished I had been there the first time they learned that lesson. Made sense; a waterproof watch isn't cheap when you make six bucks a day.

We climbed walls, slipped through cracks, and swam across deep pools. Some chambers opened wide like cathedrals; others narrowed so tight we had to shimmy through one at a time. Out of everyone in the group, I was evidently the only one feeling adventurous. I agreed to follow the guide up a rock wall to a ledge where we could jump into the water below.

The plan was this: jump, then use your momentum to dive under a submerged rock and come up on the other side of the cavern.

He jumped first. Took longer to surface than I expected, but eventually popped up near the opposite wall. I didn't hesitate. The water was pitch black, but I swam down, found the opening with my hands, and pushed off the bottom to slide through.

Then I stopped.

Fuck.

I was stuck. Underwater. Arms pinned to my sides. The guide was maybe 5'5" and 140 pounds soaking wet. I was 6', 190, and lean— just not lean enough.

The panic hit fast. But so did the instinct to act. I calmed down as much as I could and did something that made no

24

logical sense—I exhaled. Let a bunch of air out of my lungs. I remember thinking — this is either the dumbest move of my life or the only one that's going to work. But it was the only shot I had. Make myself smaller. Slide back out.

My lungs screamed. My world narrowed. I was nothing but a pinpoint of focus.

Then—sand. I felt the bottom again. Feet planted. I launched upward.

The thing about cave water is nothing lives in it. Just black rainwater dripping down for centuries. The sand was beautiful—grainy, pure, like it had been sifted through a sieve.

When I broke the surface, my eyes were saucers. I immediately locked eyes with a girl sitting on the side of the cave. No panic. No concern. No emotion. Nobody had any idea what just happened.

Based on their posture, it probably would've taken two full minutes before anyone thought to check on me.

I took a huge breath. Smiled. Said nothing.

Just got back in line and kept moving forward.

Laughing hysterically on the inside.

Nobody knew what happened under that rock. But I did. And ever since, I've walked into darkness differently.

Machete Logic

*There's no logic when a blade's involved. Just instinct, silence, and
what happens next.*
—Machete Logic

One of the funny things about living in El Salvador was that I
never had what we'd call a "normal" bedtime. Most nights I
was wiped out and in bed before nine. But every now and
then, when the mood was right and Lalo's Café was full, I'd
stay out until 2:00 or 3:00 in the morning.

Lalo was a sharp guy just a few years younger than me. He
and his crew had nowhere to hang out after the market closed
around 8 p.m. So, after asking his mom for a little space, he
packed four small tables, some chairs, and a gas stove into a
12'x30' room at the back of their house. Stocked some beer
and sandwiches, and just like that, he had a monopoly on the
nightlife outside the campo- *the fields.*

One night, after a visit to a small town south of El Roble—
Samuel showed up with a bottle of chaparro—evil homemade
liquor that kicks like a mule. Around 2:30 a.m., another friend,

Rafa, and I started wrestling. Nothing serious, just roughhousing. Rafa was ex-special forces, trained at the infamous School of the Americas, and a stone-cold killer in the war. We got along famously.

Seeing the action, my roommate Samuel jumped in and I started horsing around with him while Rafa went inside for water. That's when a short guy walked up from the street, saw us wrestling, and thought it was a real fight. Before I could explain, Cesar, my neighbor— a guy I generally kept a distance from—stepped out of the shadows and launched into the scene. He threw the guy off the curb onto his face.

Now, curbs in Latin America aren't like curbs in the U.S. At Lalo's, where the road sloped down about four feet, the curb stayed the same height. So, this guy wasn't tossed off a three-inch edge—he was launched off a four-foot drop. His face was a wreck, and he disappeared into the shadows.

That was enough excitement for one night. Samuel and I called it, and headed home.

The next day I ran into Cesar and we started chatting about what happened. Turns out the guy who got tossed, went home, grabbed a machete, and came looking for revenge. Not seeing me, he went after Cesar. Fearing for his life, Cesar picked up a rock and smashed him in the face. The guy dropped the blade, clutching his face. Cesar grabbed it and cracked him over the head with the flat side. Out cold.

That next night, there was a big dance for the town festival. The mayor had hired a band from the capital. I asked Cesar if he or I needed to be worried about retribution. He smiled, lifted his shirt to show a gun tucked in his waistband, and said, "No. I talked to my cousin. If that guy shows up, we're going to kill him."

My mind flashed. *Oh fuck.*

He crossed the street, calm as ever.

My brain was on fire. *Should I try to find the guy and explain? Should I talk to Cesar? Should I just stay home?*

Fortunately, the skies opened up like they only do in Central America. The dance was rained out. Two days later, Samuel said word on the street was that the whole thing had blown over. No deaths.

A few days after that, the police showed up at Cesar's. The guy with the twice-smashed face had filed a complaint and wanted a few hundred dollars. I watched from across the street as the officers asked Cesar to come out. The steel gate across his front door could stop a tank. He looked them dead in the eye and said, "No."

They asked for his gun. Again: "No."

An awkward standoff followed. No one moved. Then the cops left.

End of story.

By then, it was the third time my life had been directly threatened.

It's strange how casually death walked past us that night.
Not for the first time.
Not for the last.

Stamped at Dawn

It wasn't fear that got me moving, it was the math; stay and disappear. Go and maybe make it.
—Stamped at Dawn

Rain pattered lightly on the tin roof above me. Twenty minutes earlier, just before four in the morning, I had slipped out of a cockroach-infested shanty hotel somewhere deep in the Amazon in Brazil. Like most slum housing across South America, it was cinderblock with a steel door and a mosquito-ringed showerhead.

I'd arrived before dark to avoid any riffraff that might emerge after sunset. After a quick rinse—half shower, half mosquito swatting session—I ducked under the covers and pulled the sheets over my head like a makeshift mosquito net. The puke green walls matched the grime.

Just after four, I walked through a closed market without incident and paid a man sleeping in his boat a couple bucks to ferry me a few hundred yards across the water to a small cluster of floating houses somewhere in the dark. Even with a roof overhead, water crept through the seams of the boat. I was soaked before we reached the landing.

My target was a 4:30 a.m. pickup on a ferry coming downriver from Peru. The recent rains had swelled the Amazon to its highest level in recorded history. Old boat routes were gone—swallowed by the flood.

The landing looked like a movie set. A dozen incandescent bulbs flickered above the docks, throwing warped shadows on the planks and water. This tiny floating village—maybe 30 homes all tied together by 2x6s—rose and fell rhythmically with the current.

A diesel chug broke the dark. A sleek, V-hulled emerged with 50 passengers—my ride.

Or so I thought.

A short man stepped off the stern and came directly toward me. In Spanish, he asked for my passport. He saw immediately I hadn't been stamped into Peru—though I'd been stamped out of Brazil earlier that day. I had been told there was a place to get the entry stamp here in the floating village. Technically, I was standing in the middle of the Amazon, straddling two countries.

"No good," the captain said. He started prepping the boat to leave.

Normally, this would just mean a delay—an extra day of travel, maybe some hammock time. But there was no way back to the mainland. And the three rough-looking men sitting about 20 yards to my left seemed to take a keen interest in the situation. One of them was openly playing with a long knife on a table.

I didn't like the math. Gringo. Isolated. No witnesses. Backpack full of gear. With the floods this bad, if a body went into the river, it wouldn't come out for months—if ever.

The rain picked up, soaking my head and shoulders. My pulse pounded as heat rose into face.

I stepped toward the captain, voice lower but firmer now, asking—then demanding—to be let on the boat. He refused. Said he had a schedule to keep. Then he adjusted his shirt, just enough to reveal a chrome .45 on his belt.

Kindly, he mentioned the Peruvian immigration officer actually slept in one of the huts. One of the men holding the boat offered to take me to find him. The captain agreed to wait.

Through a maze of huts and sagging wires, we rode in a dugout canoe. The rain blurred the edges of everything. I kept my eyes ahead and on the man behind me. Adrenaline humming.

We reached the hut. I knocked lightly at first. Nothing. My guide suggested we give up.

But years earlier, before skydiving over the Caribbean, I learned a trick about fear. You can't out-think it. You won't calm your heart. Best thing is to focus *entirely* on the task at hand. Just do the next thing.

So I kept knocking.

I'm scrappy, 6'0", 195 lbs. I can defend myself. But maybe not against three guys and a knife, in the dark, over fast-moving water. My odds weren't good.

So, I knocked louder. Pounded with fists. Kicked the door. Either the officer was dead, or not home. But I kept knocking, partly to buy time. I needed a plan B. Use my backpack as a shield, maybe push the guys off the dock, steal a canoe, and cross before dawn.

Then the door opened.

The immigration officer stood there, bleary-eyed. I nearly hugged him. I apologized, slid him a $10 tip, and under candlelight, he stamped me into Peru.

We'd been gone maybe 20 minutes. My odds of the boat still waiting felt slim. I asked my driver to take me to the mainland, but he refused. Too dangerous in the dark.

Didn't matter.

The boat was still there.

The three men at the dock watched in silence as I boarded. My heart was thumping. I felt a full-body wave of relief, gratitude, and the strange joy that only comes when you truly think you might not make it.

It felt so good to be alive.
And the real adventure was just beginning.

Amazon Boat Adventure

Whatever happened next, it was going to be the best moment of my life—because they were getting out, even if it meant I didn't make it.
—Amazon Boat Adventure

After narrowly making it back onto the boat in *Stamped at Dawn*, soaked and buzzing with adrenaline, I thought the worst was behind me. I'd managed to talk my way through immigration, dodge a sketchy standoff, and climb aboard a ferry drifting in a flooded Amazon between Brazil and Peru. Relief washed over me—briefly.

Because now, the real ride began.

The boat headed to Iquitos was packed. About 60 passengers, four crew members, and exactly four life jackets. The air was thick and stale. The windows were tiny slits tucked near the rotted fiberglass roof. We sat so low in the water it felt less like a vessel and more like a floating coffin.

I couldn't help but scan for escape routes. The only door—the front hatch—looked like it weighed four tons by the way the crew manhandled it. The woman next to me, a heavy breather with questionable survival prospects, was spilling into my space. I made mental notes: she wouldn't fit through the window. Behind me were three kids. If this boat went down, I was getting them to the surface. That much I knew. Whatever happened next, it was going to be the best moment of my life—because they were coming with me, even if it meant I didn't make it.

Some people might've felt reassured that the captain was holding a flashlight out the side window to steer. I wasn't one of them. His instrument panel was dead. The main floodlight didn't work. The only light came from his arm.

The Amazon was in full flood. Trees, debris, rooftops—everything was half-submerged. The tops of houses had become the new speed bumps.

I was about to shift in my seat—partly to brace my legs, partly to reclaim some space—when we slammed into something. The engine coughed, sputtered, and died.

Rain pounded the boat. We turned gently in the current and began tilting against the river's flow. The silence was thick. So was the dark. I mentally rehearsed grabbing the kids and pushing them up through the hatch. I knew if we got to shore the jungle wouldn't let up.

I wore my boots tight. Not because I was tough— the opposite. Stepping onto that jungle floor barefoot would've stopped my heart. And with the flood, the trees were crawling with snakes getting out of the water. The day before, I'd been on the back of a motorcycle with a Brazilian girl showing me

around town. She had pointed out places the locals avoid—
"*Anacondas live there,*" she'd said, matter-of-fact.

Then, out of nowhere, I thought—*God, one more blowjob
would've been nice.*
It was absurd, but that's what surfaced. In the middle of real
fear, my brain served up a parting wish— no glory, no deep
final thoughts. Just one more laughable, very human craving.

As if responding to the captain's cursing, the engine turned
over. The moment passed. The hatch swung open. Rain came
in soaking me, but I smiled the remainder of the ride. Not just
because we were moving again. But because I still had
something to want.

I'd skydived before work once in Puerto Rico. Twice, actually.
Signed a waiver that said YOU MAY DIE in all caps. I thought
that was living on the edge. But at least when you jump out of
a plane, you expect to fall. You're strapped in. You choose the
fear.

This? This was different. You're not in control. You're just alive
until you're not.

And still—there's something beautiful in it. There's
something freeing in being pushed to the edge, feeling
everything, and laughing in the rain as it soaks your bones.

We weren't even halfway to Iquitos. And already, the jungle
had reminded me how lucky I was to still be here.

Walk at the End of the Earth

I had no tent, no sleeping bag, no way back. Just forward.
—Walk at the End of the Earth

As I turned in my passport at the Brazilian embassy in Santiago, Chile, the man behind the counter told me it would take seven days to process the visa. With time to kill and no passport, I booked a flight to Punta Arenas, on the tip of South America.

I arrived in the morning and wandered the city center before catching a bus to Puerto Natales, a small town on the edge of a national park. Its namesake: four jagged granite towers, the Torres del Paine. The light gray stone—framed by black sedimentary caps—caught the sun and scattered it over a pristine lake, like nature showing off.

Pressed for time, I joined a senior citizens' bus tour through the park. The following evening, back at the hostel, stiff and hungry, I wanted only a shower and food—but I couldn't help but be drawn in by the windburned hikers gathered outside the pub. Their eyes were bright. Their arms swept wide as they recounted stories. Their words carried the weight of wild terrain.

That night, quietly, I decided I couldn't let this place pass through me. I would hike it. Alone.

Early the next morning, I took a three-hour bus into the wilderness and caught a boat across a glacial lake the color of clouded topaz. As I stepped off the dock, a man at the ranger station eyed my pack.

"Hey man, your pack looks light. Do you have a tent?"

No.

"A sleeping bag?"

No.

"You know the ferry doesn't come back until noon tomorrow, right?"

Yeah, I know, I thought. Cortés probably burned his boats on a day like this.

He said something else, but the wind—which hasn't ceased for millennia—ripped his words away. He probably mentioned my clothes weren't up to the task. That was also obvious. But I figured worst-case, I'd do air squats and push-ups every 15 minutes to stay warm through the night.

Patagón means "bigfoot" in Spanish. Magellan gave the region its name after spotting enormous footprints along the shore in the 1500s. Why anyone chose to stay and build lives in this wind-blasted, teeth-baring corner of the earth is beyond me. My throat tightened as I looked out over the emptiness.

A dry smile crossed my lips. Just yesterday I'd given my map to a Spanish gentleman who'd lost his on the bus tour.

The hike was long and, at times, treacherous. One wrong step and you'd find yourself dangling off a cliff—or worse. My pack was light. I hadn't brought water either— luckily the mountain streams were clear and cold.

After hours of battling headwinds, I reached the last outpost: a ranger station at Lake Grey, home to one of the most stunning glaciers in the southern hemisphere. The station was spacious and empty. Eventually, the ranger returned. Casually—like I was asking for a spare cigarette—I asked if he had a tent and sleeping bag I could rent.

He laughed. Then realized I was serious. He disappeared out back for what felt like forever.

While I waited, I considered how I might phrase my request to the French girl I'd met on the trail—would she let a total stranger stay in her tent? At least we'd be warm. A grin crept in.

The ranger returned, smiling, and $30 later I had gear. I stuffed my things into the tent and stitched up a gaping hole in my pants—the handiwork of a flirty tree branch from earlier that day.

But I wasn't done. I hadn't come this far to miss the glacier. It was still two hours away. The sun would set in two and a half. The odds weren't in my favor.

I walked toward the tent, dejected. The thought of getting lost in Patagonia at night without food, gear, a light, or compass sobered me. A little.

Then I decided to run.

Running instead of walking cut the time nearly in half. I made it. I stood alone in silence, watching the last sunlight dance across the ancient blue ice. And then I ran back.

That night, I collapsed into my tent, exhausted and full. I even slept a few hours before the cold woke me and stayed to gnaw at my toes until dawn.

The next morning, I hiked back slowly. When the boat captain saw me, he gave a knowing nod as I boarded. I slumped into my seat, wrecked but lit up. An irrepressible smile crept across my windburned face.
My heart was full — not with triumph, but something quieter.
Something like arrival.

That night, I kept moving forward.

Forward is a direction, not a feeling.

And years later, when the path ahead feels cold and unclear, I still think of that wind and ice.

Long Walk – Managua, Nicaragua

We were two travelers, half-sure of everything, full of sweat and silence and maybe some grace.
—Long Walk

Sweat dripped from my brow. Hours earlier, I gave up trying to peel my shirt from my lats as I walked through the Nicaraguan night. Images of Reagan and Oliver North swirled in my head. Until that day, America's impact on this region lived only in TV clips and childhood headlines. But as we passed a famous bronze statue of a soldier holding an AK-47 overhead—arms stretched wide in symbolic defiance—my eyes widened. Holy shit, I thought. This was cool. The figure was oddly proportioned— stout, immovable. Like someone who could be lost in a crowd but never shaken from the earth.

Dark had fallen just a couple hours earlier, yet the streets were already desolate—like a cold Alaskan winter night. Along the road sat a shantytown of lean-tos and patched-together shelters, shielded by little more than a chain-link fence. A few hours earlier, I would've rushed past this place. But tonight, it was home. The bugs were unavoidable, but that was a different matter.

Earlier that day, Tono—a solemn Salvadoran friend with a soft spot for big, loud women—and I took a bus from El Salvador down to Nicaragua, chasing adventure. I never expected to find myself in a jungle where English, not Spanish, was the lingua franca, hearing someone say, "There are no roads to that place," and realizing we were out of money.

Tono's girlfriend lived in Chinandega, home to the Flor de Caña rum distillery. We first stopped in Managua to visit her family—in a slum pressed against a mall built after hundreds of families had been displaced.

Their home was a 20x20' three-bedroom hovel, seemingly supported only by the neighboring units. A woman— presumably Tono's mother-in-law—greeted us with a grin as wide as her hips and immediately began frying plantains. Her laughter cracked the air, drawing rare smiles from the usually impassive Tono. We were in good hands.

Her husband seemed kind, too. A recovering alcoholic who admitted to sleeping just two or three hours a night, he worked as a baggage handler at the international airport. My gut told me he was both trustworthy and intimately familiar with life's harsher realities. Maybe he was the man behind the AK.

After an hour of rest, we set off on foot to tour downtown Managua—a journey that would take us miles. To save the bus fare, we hoofed it. I splurged later at the lakefront, buying three tickets for a wildlife cruise. Ripples danced across the

41

water's surface, and birds of every color stitched the sky. It felt good.

At a supermarket stop, I loaded a week's worth of food into our arms—just enough for the three of us to carry on the two-hour walk back. The home had two beds: one for the 16-year-old son (to whom we gave a new soccer ball), and one for the parents. Despite our objections, Tono and I were given the parents' bed. They split the couch and recliner that night.

The bed was awful. Probably older than me. Getting up early was easy.

We caught the last two seats on a bus headed east—Tono somewhere in the middle, me smushed into a rigid seat in the back with two chickens and a pile of produce. Nine hours later, we stumbled off into thick jungle air.

There, we found a dugout canoe driver willing to take us two hours downriver to Bluefields. As we skimmed through the forest's arteries, we passed houses perched on stilts so tall they looked like treehouses. The breeze off the river kept the early heat at bay. For a moment, everything was perfect.

Bluefields deserves its own story, so I'll save it.

Our final stop was back in Chinandega, in an apartment four stories up overlooking an unpaved street. Luz, a 19-year-old with a hard frame and a mane of tight brown curls, took immediate interest in the gringo. She found endless reasons to bend over in front of me, drawing the attention of both travelers.

At first, I thought it was a game—until her sister stepped out of the room, and Luz stepped in. She pressed into me with a playful hug, flashed her perfect teeth, and whispered too fast to catch.

After the slums, the jungle, and a thousand miles of heat and hunger, of course I was still moved by something as simple as a glance. There's no use pretending otherwise — the pull of human connection is ancient, almost animal. It's not weakness. It's proof we're still alive. Tono, ever the cool observer, nodded from across the room, arms folded in silent approval.

As Luz slid out just before her sister returned, a sly smile played at the edge of her lips, peeking over her shoulder.

As I imagined, my adventure with her was just beginning...

It ended the next morning. While I was in the bathroom, Luz helped herself to the contents of my backpack and wallet. Every last cordoba and dollar—gone. Tono and I had to beg our way back across the border. Back to another country—pockets empty, pride in tatters, sunburned, and laughing.

The real lesson wasn't about Luz. It was that every journey comes with a price — and the payment isn't always in cash.

Tacos and Wreckage

I smiled big. Not because I was okay — but because I saw what was coming, and let it come anyway.
—Tacos and Wreckage

Whole Foods in Austin is nuts.
It's the HQ—the mothership—and it shows.

On weekends, I take my girl there for breakfast—the kind of mornings that make dating her feel like cheating the system. She heads off to grab salsa for our tacos while I snag a cozy seat near the escalator, facing the window.

She's about 30 yards away now, scanning. I raise my arm above the mostly seated crowd and wave—slowly, like a beacon. I'm happy. She's awesome, and I'm excited to be spending the morning with her.

Then—out of nowhere—*one of my former kills enters the scene.* She sees me waving.

She starts walking toward me.
She thinks I'm flagging her down.

It's like watching a car crash in slow motion. Both women are closing in—smiling, steps apart. One carrying salsa. The other, a memory.

I smile big—genuine—but with full recognition of the catastrophe unfolding.

It's a beautiful day. Whole Foods is alive with people easing into their mornings over eggs and green juice. None of them know they're moments away from being splattered with profanity, tacos, and those impossibly tiny salsa cups.

The two couldn't be more different.

The skeleton is a professional singer. Tall. Raven-haired. Thin enough to slip through shadows. She rarely smiles. Just stares— those pool-dark eyes. She has an antique clawfoot tub that saw things one night even Ron Jeremy couldn't narrate.

My girl—blonde, about 5'4"—is quick to smile. Razor-sharp. Incandescently smart. I wouldn't trade her for anything.

Holy fuck.

The singer's eyes widen as she gets close. The corner of her mouth curls—maybe a smile, maybe a smirk. For half a second, I think: at least she remembers me fondly.

Then my girl—the blonde—says, "Oh shit."

The hairs on the back of my neck go full porcupine.

For a heartbeat, I think she sees it all. But no—she forgot something. Salsa emergency. She spins and heads back to the bar.

I laugh—hard—and pivot just enough to shift our angle. The singer takes two extra steps, and now we're side by side—primed for her to keep moving.

We exchange a few lines while the salsa gods keep the keeper occupied.

She catches the scent immediately.
Like any fox, she only needs a whiff.
 She leans in, drops, "We should get together sometime," over her shoulder, and vanishes into the crowd.

I don't say anything, but the voice in my head is clear: *No way—I've got my keeper.*

I ate about 40 tacos after that.

Part III—Mortality & Meaning

The body breaks. The world turns. And something deeper takes root.

A Reprieve, but No Pardon

Death has more patience than life. You may escape him for a day, or many years, but there is no pardon.
— Don Trush

I was young once, but woke up late and realized I'm dancing at twilight.
— Saturday Jefferson

I never thought I'd own a pair of weightlifting shoes. But there I was — laced into my new Nike Pumps, tears running, Pantera's *Cowboys from Hell* screaming from the speakers. What the hell had just happened? And how did I have any right to be mad?

Nobody wants to tell you that you've got a tumor in your neck. Not even the doctors. They'll call it a *mass* or a *lump* and stall for time. Sometimes they hand the conversation to a Resident — "for training" — just to avoid eye contact.
But Google doesn't lie. Not this time.

The day before, I went in for my annual checkup — the usual song and dance: doctor tells me my cholesterol's high, I nod, promise to do better, we both act like that's care.
Except this time I told him I'd been doing PT for three months and the pain in my neck hadn't budged.
Dry needling, exercises — nothing.
And while the PT wasn't hard on the eyes, I was all set doing things that didn't work.

I mentioned a bump I could feel, just above the collarbone, in front of my trap. He felt it, and somehow got me an ultrasound the next day.

So, there I was, shirtless, on a paper-covered table, neck cranked sideways trying to see the screen.
The tech stopped, went to get the radiologist.
As soon as the door closed, I snapped a photo of the image, put on a smile, and waited.

Out in the parking lot, I Googled it.
Tumors — "masses" with blood flow activity.
I didn't know what those looked like, but the screen in my pocket sure as hell matched what Google showed me.

I brought the photo home and showed my wife.

Now, she's a physician. Sharp. Steady. Has seen a lot.
But she didn't say anything. She just turned and walked upstairs.

Confused, I stood in the kitchen, grabbed a glass of water, then went to find her.
She was in bed, crying into a box of tissues.

She apologized. Said she didn't want me to see her break —
said she needed to stay strong.
But fuck that. We needed a realignment.

I told her: strong isn't pretending. Strong is falling apart and
rebuilding, together.
Strong is crying *with* someone.
That's the real stuff. That's what pulls us closer.

So, I did what I could. I laced up my lifting shoes and got after
it.
Enderton's home lifting program. If my days were numbered,
I wasn't about to skip front squats.

Midway through the session, my doctor called.
He was surprised by my tone.

Said the radiologist confirmed the lump needed more
imaging. He was still holding back.
So I told him — I saw the blood flow on the screen. I knew
what this probably was.
He agreed: we'd move fast.

My wife was already regrouping. She suggested I drive into
Boston — Mass Eye and Ear had an urgent care.
Why wait? It was less than an hour away.

So, I threw on a hoodie, got in the car, and let Pantera roar the
whole ride in.

Mass Eye and Ear — those people are quiet heroes. They got
me in, ran tests, and finished with a fine needle aspiration —
FNA — where they jam a hollow needle five or six times into
the mass to pull samples for the lab.

I didn't make a sound. But I broke into a full sweat.
It felt like my arm had grabbed a Tesla charger — electricity

down the nerves, hand on fire.
I kept breathing slow. Zoomed out. Detached.

The doctor finished the first needle and said, "Okay, five or six more pokes."
LFG.

Later we learned the tumor was in my nerve.
She was stabbing it directly.
That explains the white flashes.

It reminded me of a trip years earlier, when my back blew out and I couldn't stand for five days.
Then the pain vanished — but my leg didn't work.
My wife rushed me to the ER, and by dumb luck one of the best spine surgeons in the country was practicing in San Antonio.
Wednesday consult. Thursday pre-op. Friday surgery.
He told me if we'd waited till Monday, I might never have recovered. Another close call.

Anyway — back to the neck — the FNA was inconclusive. So, they scheduled an MRI.
That took weeks to get.
The MRI? Also, inconclusive.

By then I was living in a weird kind of limbo.
No diagnosis, no plan, no timeline.
Just... waiting.

Eventually I saw a neurosurgeon. He wasn't sure what to do — couldn't operate without taking the nerve, which would take the use of my left arm with it.
And here's the kicker: I'm left-handed.
Losing that arm wouldn't have just sucked — it would've

changed everything. Writing, lifting, hugging my kids — all of it.

So, he sent me to oncology.

Somewhere in the middle of that stretch — between the inconclusive scans and the big unknown — I flew to Johns Hopkins for a second opinion.
Caught the 6am to Baltimore. Sat at the harbor with a coffee, just looking out at the sky.
I had time to wander into the National Aquarium. Watched the sharks. Let my brain float.

Then I went to my appointment. The doctor was phenomenal — kind, thoughtful, unhurried. Just *there*.
Afterward, I still had time to hit a hot yoga class nearby.

As I was leaving, the teacher asked how my day was.
I laughed and said, "I flew in from Boston to see a specialist at Johns Hopkins. Your class just brightened a really tough day."

She beamed but didn't say a word.
Didn't need to.

That started another waiting period. It had been a couple months by now.
During that time, we kept going — kids, work, life.
But under the surface, we were sitting in purgatory.

And what's strange is, while all that was happening, the world just kept spinning.

I remember going out to dinner with friends in Boston — one of those breezy, light-hearted nights.
Someone asked, "Did you get your wife something special for her birthday?"

They didn't know what was going on behind the scenes. None of them did.

I smiled and said, "Yeah, actually. I already booked her a surprise trip — she's flying to Dallas to spend the weekend with her two best friends."

And it was true. We'd planned it a month in advance — before the MRI, before the waiting really stretched out.
I figured — if everything went sideways, at least she'd get that weekend.

We had to wait another week after seeing oncology to get the PET scan.
It was scheduled for Friday.

That week, while I was lifting — again — I got a call from Richie, the husband of one of my wife's friends from residency. She'd quietly reached out to her circle, just looking for help, insight, anything.

Richie and I exchanged the usual pleasantries, then I said it — not dramatically, just honestly:
"Richie, I've lived a good life."

He didn't hesitate. In his Irish brogue he said,
"No, no, no, man. We're going to get through this and laugh about it in a year over a glass of wine."

And it hit me. Not because I fully believed him, but because I needed someone to.

That Friday morning, I woke at 4:30, did my front squats, and headed to the scan.
They injected me with radioactive dye so the PET images would light up like a Christmas tree if anything else was hiding inside me.

Afterward, my wife headed straight to the airport for her birthday trip. I told her to go, to have fun, to *live* — because what else could we do?

I stayed back and took my three daughters to Disney on Ice with my middle brother.
I sat there, next to my girls, watching their faces light up — and felt completely, utterly surreal.
I had radioactive material coursing through my blood. I was wondering if I'd ever see a show like this again.

But they were laughing. Smiling.
And in that moment, I felt so much joy I could barely hold it in.

We even got a perfect parking spot — one block from TD Garden with just enough time on the meter.
Huge win.

Through it all, my parents and siblings were incredibly supportive.
Everyone carried the weight with us — silently, steadily.
My sister was in the Peace Corps in Guatemala, sending prayers and strength from a world away.
My parents, especially, didn't try to fix it with words — they just showed up.
They taught me that sometimes what matters most isn't what you say.
It's how you keep moving when things feel like they might stop.

My wife came home Sunday night.
We got the results Monday morning.

Clean.

No other tumors. Just the one.

Eventually we found Dr. Brooks — a specialist in nerve-related surgery, defined by quite compassion and extraordinary skill. After a few months of planning, he performed the operation.

Afterward, he told me it had gotten hairy in there. He couldn't get at the tumor without risking my arm.
So he did something rare. He stopped. Sat down. Regrouped.
Then tried a different approach.
And just like that, the tumor popped out.

No damage. No compromise.
Later — in a weird twist of fate — he hired my wife to work in his practice.

All in, it took months.
Months of not knowing. Of pretending everything was fine while people complained about traffic or cold coffee or whether the oat milk was foamed right.

I didn't say anything. I just nodded.
But inside, I felt different.
And even now — I hardly complain. Or try not to.
Because when you walk through that kind of fog, and come out the other side, every day feels like a favor.

Just to be clear — I'm not calling myself a cancer survivor.
I was lucky.
I got a reprieve.
But that brush with the void? It changed me.

I'm grateful. Grateful to hug my kids. Laugh with my wife.
Write these dispatches.

And yeah, maybe lace up my weightlifting shoes and sweat
through another set — because I still can.

Rafa Leaves for America

He walked two hours a day to guard a mayor. He'd survived war, but not cousins.

—Rafa Leaves for America

One afternoon I received a call from an elated Rafa. He was a wiry Salvadoran man, tall by local standards, maybe just shy of forty. Since the Salvadorean civil war, he'd worked as the mayor's bodyguard—a role he filled with paradoxical cheer and quiet authority. He always packed a Glock, though you'd hardly notice— except for the occasional awkward bulge under his shirt. Rafa was almost always smiling. First to sing at birthday parties. First to dance. I never once heard him complain or speak poorly of anyone—which was remarkable considering he walked nearly two hours each way to work.

He called to tell me he was heading north to the U.S.–Mexico border. His plan was to slip across and make his way to California, where his cousins lived. I had no doubt he'd make it. I smiled at the thought of him doing something clandestine—it felt ironic. Rafa was a proud graduate of the U.S. Army's School of the Americas. He'd been trained by Green Berets to shoot, skydive, scuba dive, survive off the land, and kill. During the Salvadoran civil war, he'd been one of the elites.

He didn't talk about it often, but once in a while—like when the mayor toured town—he'd give someone a quiet, thousand-yard stare. Just enough to let you know what he was capable of. Then, as quickly as it came, he'd be laughing again. The memory of the killer vanished.

Once, we were flying down the highway behind the mayor's pickup. Rafa sat up on the side rail of the bed, one leg dangling over, foot braced on the bumper. He steadied himself, then aimed an imaginary pistol at us. Eyes dead cold—like a hunter.
For a second, it felt like staring through the crosshairs of war itself—straight through our souls.
Rafa had seen combat. Real combat. He wasn't playing. And in that moment, you could feel it—something unspoken, something earned and endured.
His windbreaker flapped violently in the wind, but he was still. Poised. A cat in freeze-frame, singularly focused. Ready to pounce.

I can still see it—his face stripped of all emotion. Not cold. Not angry. Just... hollow.
Impressive. Earned. Sacred.

He lived with his mother in a humble two-room home in the country. It was sparsely furnished, with a wood-fire stove and a hammock swinging on the front porch. Still, it felt deeply lived in. One time, when we stopped there on our way to hike in the woods, his mother served us plantain soup. I remember the taste. I remember the warmth.

In El Salvador, it's bad luck to tell anyone but your closest family that you're heading north illegally. Nobody likes to jinx a lottery ticket. By contrast, those who had visas made sure to remind everyone, as often as possible, that they were holders of such sacred stamps.

So, I didn't get the call until Rafa was already en route. We'd struck up an unexpectedly close friendship during our time working together, but I was still surprised he told anyone. As was the custom, I kept my mouth shut until the next day, when I shared his goodbye quietly with friends in the mayor's office and the coconut guy down by the edge of town—one of the most popular hangouts.

As expected, he arrived safely and found work quickly. I looked forward to seeing him again—maybe in LA, with the rest of the crew—when I eventually went home.

That's why it hit so hard when they shipped his body back in a black casket only a few months later.

Word on the street was that there had been an argument in the apartment with his cousins. They said he was grabbed from behind, fell awkwardly into the refrigerator, and broke his neck.

God knows the truth, and that ain't it.

He and I had drilled what to do if grabbed from behind. We used to scrap all the time—in the mayor's office after work, on the asphalt out front, whenever there was space. Rafa was thin, but he was tough—real tough. He knew a ton. His balance, his instincts, his strength-to-weight ratio—you'd never move him unless he wanted to be moved. Unless his cousin was twice my size, Rafa didn't go down like that.

His mother had to pay $3,000—a year's salary—to bring him home. The man in the box looked small. Frail. It was a sad day.

Shortly after the funeral, I went to the capital to print every photo I had with Rafa in it. His mother had been too poor to ever take pictures of her own son.

So, I gave her mine.

The Arc in My Skull

We all make mistakes we can't take back. And sooner or later, we all hope to be forgiven for something.
—The Arc in My Skull

In college, I was a resident assistant — supposed to be responsible, available, present. One night, after my shift technically ended, I slipped out to visit some friends. I figured I'd be gone half an hour. It turned into three days.

There was a party. Two guys started to fight. I stepped between them. One of them had a pint glass in his hand. He smashed it into my head.

The glass left a dent in the wall — even after hitting my skull.

I don't remember the sound — only the weight, and the sudden warmth as blood poured down my neck. There were guys at the party who helped — pressing against the wound, keeping me upright, staying calm when it mattered.

I spent a few days in the hospital, hovering just shy of brain surgery. When they wheeled me in, I was covered in blood.

They cut away my shirt. Pulled down my pants. I wasn't wearing underwear. One of the nurses — young, probably just a few years older than me — averted her eyes and turned away quickly, with quiet modesty. There was no shame in it. Just respect. I couldn't help but smile inside.

The head nurse came back later, smirked, and said, "You should come back when you're better — I'll set you up with her."
I was bandaged, bruised, and half-conscious... but I remember laughing. That kind of gesture — the small kindness, the human nudge — it meant more than I could've said.

I still have a visible dent in my skull — the arc of the glass etched into bone. It's permanent.

I never held it against the guy who hit me. He was dumb. Drunk. Angry. Young. We all make mistakes we can't take back. And sooner or later, we all hope to be forgiven for something.

I returned to school not long after. My dormitory manager — knowing I technically wasn't supposed to be off campus — ignored it. Another small grace.

There's no clean moral to the story. Just a mark on my head. A few days missing. And a deeper understanding of how fragile things are — and how much strength there is in the people who hold you up while you bleed.

Torch to Carry

I'll give it to you straight: you probably need brain surgery.
—Torch to Carry

It started on one of those almost-too-perfect August days. We were driving from Massachusetts to Vermont for a family vacation, under a massive blue sky peppered with puffy white clouds—the kind you see on blustery summer days that feel almost too big to hold. I eased off the highway, pulled into a Burger King parking lot, and asked my mom to take over driving. My two older kids—ages six and three—sat in the back, munching on seaweed snacks. My mom looked at me with that silent mom-check, the one that says, *something's wrong,* but didn't ask questions.

I'd been feeling it for about 45 minutes. A headache—not just a dull ache, but a kettle-on-the-boil kind of pressure rising behind my eyes. I cycled through tricks— A/C on, windows down, neck roll, slow breathing. Nothing helped. I didn't want to scare the kids, but by the time we stopped, I knew I had to act.

As soon as she sat down behind the wheel, I said, "Mom, I'm sorry, but you need to take me to the hospital."

She didn't blink. Just pulled back onto the road and headed for the hospital over the bridge. It rose into view—stark and sterile—as we crested the hill.

Inside the ER, the air was heavy with fluorescent light and a kind of shapeless waiting. An agitated couple sat by the window. A woman in a wheelchair looked like her body had given up long before she did. I stepped up to the desk and said quietly, "I need help."

The woman didn't look up. Took my name. Asked me to wait.

A few minutes later, someone else brought me around to the check-in desk. She glanced at my ID, noted my changed address, and said they'd seen me before. Over 20 years ago. Skull fracture. Pint glass. Ambulance ride.

"What's going on today?" she asked.

"My head feels like it's going to explode."

Usually, I look healthy—fit, even. But something in my voice must've registered. She picked up the phone. A gurney rolled out almost instantly.

The doctor came straight over. "What's going on?"

"Feels like my head is going to explode."

That was enough. They paged a transport team. CAT scan at the main hospital. Possible ruptured aneurysm. No time to lose.

I called my mom. Told her calmly they were moving me. She followed behind the ambulance with my girls, keeping it together for them while quietly falling apart inside.

Funny contrast: the girls watching the lights with wide-eyed excitement, and my mom white-knuckling the steering wheel.

At the hospital, I was whisked into a room. Tests. IV. No wasted motion. They slid me into the scanner, and as soon as I went in, I was coming back out.

They moved me to a private room. The head ER doc asked everyone else to leave. He pulled up a stool and sat at the foot of the bed.

"You don't look like a bullshitter," he said. "And I'm not a bullshitter either. So, I'll give it to you straight: you probably need brain surgery. We're going to heli-vac you to Boston to see Dr. Ogilvy. He's the best. I've got him on speed dial. We'll know more in a few minutes. If you want to call anyone, **now's the time**." He said those last three words slow and emphatically.

My fantasy football draft was in a week.

No. I didn't think that. But I also wasn't ready to check out.

First thought: my wife. She was in Kansas with our baby girl, flying out the next day to meet us in Vermont. She was probably packing while our daughter pulled socks out of the suitcase. Calling her wouldn't change anything. If this turned bad, she wouldn't make it in time.

I dialed in. "Mom, how are the girls? Good? I'm glad you got ice cream. This might take a little longer than we thought, but I'll let you know."

This was my torch to carry. For now.

Minutes later, the doctor came back. Scan was clean. I was safe.

I felt better too. They wanted me to stay, but I told them I was leaving. Vermont was calling.

We drove on. Grandma behind the wheel. I didn't say much. At the rental house, I collapsed into bed.

I spent most of that week horizontal. Being upright for more than 30 minutes triggered a wave of sickness and crushing head pain.

Back in Kansas, I saw my doctor. He ran through a checklist. Ordered an MRI. Asked if I'd had issues with my eyes or ears.

Yes. Watching motion made me dizzy. Swings, especially. And I couldn't go underwater on the left side. He referred me out.

I'm decent with people. Calm. Open. Sometimes they overshare. My doctor, half-listening, said, "Sometimes with headaches like this, the MRI lights up like a Christmas tree with little tumors."

I looked at him. Buddy, your mic's on.

He backtracked. "Of course, I don't think that'll happen in your case."

Still, I had to tell my wife. And we heard of someone—a friend-of-a-friend and father of three—who had brain cancer. We heard what it did.

I didn't think that was my path. But doubt gets loud in the silence.

MRI came back clean. So did ENT. And audiology. And ophthalmology.

Eventually, I landed in front of a physical therapist. He said I should try standing up and sitting down 30 times consecutively three times a day. Said it would "train my system." Said it worked before.

It made me violently nauseous. But I did it anyway. Religiously. I wanted out.

He was a "cash only" guy. I should've known. But when you're desperate, even a guy with a clipboard outside a van seems like hope.

Meds didn't help either.

Then my wife circled back to something we'd heard: pseudomeningocele.

Turns out she was right. I had a tear in the dura—the sheath around the spinal cord. When I stood up, cerebrospinal fluid leaked out the bottom of my back. The pressure inside my skull dropped like a fruit being pulled through a drain.

The pain was real. And it *was* in my head.

And it was my fault.

Two months earlier, I'd had emergency back surgery. I'd been in so much pain; I lived lying on the floor of my in-laws' house for five days. My surgeon said, "If we don't operate this week, you may never regain full use of your leg."

Post-op, I followed every rule. Didn't lift. Didn't twist. Sat down and had my kids brought to me.

Two months later, I was cleared. We flew to Massachusetts. I moved again. That movement likely tore the dura. Before that, the sharp bone fragment hadn't been rubbing. Now it was.

pseudomeningocele usually happen immediately after surgery. Most often in mothers who've had epidurals.

I called the surgeon. Sent him my old MRI. He confirmed it. Then said, "Can you gut it out for a few more months? It might heal on its own."

It took six.

Six months of avoiding upright life. Of lying down to stay sane. But we made it through.

My mom came to help. Again. She'd already been trapped with us for three months during COVID. She turned 70 in our house. We surprised her with giant birthday letters on the lawn. She helped with the newborn. Never complained. Just showed up.

And my wife—she carried the real load. Three kids. A job. All the heavy lifting. She lived her vows. And I'll never forget that.

Sometimes your body folds. But if you're lucky, your people don't. I am so grateful.

The Bet She Made

The meeting of two personalities is like the contact of two chemical substances: if there is any reaction, both are transformed.
— Carl Jung

By the time I met you, all of the chapters in this book had already been written — except the two most important: this one, the story of our journey, and the one about our children. But I swear I saw them twinkling in your eyes that day we met on a shaded patio deep in Texas.

We'd been introduced but hadn't really met. I walked up to the hostess stand at the Gristmill to ask where you were sitting. Before I could speak, the girl looked at me and said, "You must be him — come right this way."

I remember changing my shirt a few times before getting into my twelve-year-old Mercury to meet you. And there you were: white tee shirt, crimped hair, big smile. We ordered two Lone

Star beers — the ones with the riddles in the caps — and you solved both before I could get a word out. Ha. Whip smart. Valedictorian. We are so different. It is a perfect match.

Later, I surprised you at an airport layover en route to California, and we got engaged right there in the terminal. I was definitely nervous. "Fuck yeah, I'll marry you," was your reply. Fire meets fire. It was electric from the start. I like to joke we met in Vegas and got engaged. It's not exactly true but captures the energy.

This has been a hell of a journey. Best one yet. And we're still rolling.

From the very beginning, you saw me. Right to my core. And you went all in.

You bet on me with your future. We got engaged as I wrapped up grad school and started applying for jobs. By then, I had turned things around and graduated with a 3.7 GPA, near the top of my class. I was relentless — applying, networking, interviewing. Every time I came home, I was energized, hopeful. And you felt it too.

You got excited with me, told me to check my email. Friends from school were connecting me with bankers in Houston, oil & gas execs in San Antonio, a global real estate group in Dallas. One CEO even arranged interviews with every department head at his company just to see where I might fit.

And still, the answers came back the same: "Nice guy, but not a fit. Sorry."

The more I heard "no," the harder I tried. I hired a career coach. I earned my CFA — one of the hardest designations out there. And I owe that to you. You said, "Shit or get off the pot."

So, I studied every night while you held down the fort with two kids in diapers and a third on the way. And I passed.

Still, the rejections didn't stop. In twelve years together, I've only landed one job through a formal interview. That kind of thing wears on a person.

What I didn't see back then was that I was trying to succeed in the wrong system. I kept shaping myself to fit it — but the fit was never going to come. I wasn't wired for their mold. I was built to build something else. And somewhere deep down, I know you saw that too. That's what made it harder — knowing who I was at my core, and watching the world pass it by. You believed in me. Long before there was any proof.

It was the opposite of what you'd experienced: you thrived in school, got into medical school, matched with your top residency program. And then you had to watch me get knocked down — over and over again.

I'm sure it wore on you. How could it not?

Around the time I was rejected from a job supervising trash routes, we made a change. We moved. You found a job you loved. We were close to your dad, and I loved him too. The girls and I visited him often — even without you.

When he died, my heart broke too. Something in me shifted — like waking from a dream I didn't know I'd been inside. Not just grief, but clarity. A deep, unshakable pull from the core of my being. My dad was getting older. And I had a dream. Not your dream — mine. And I needed to go.

"This is my only chance to work with my dad," I said. "We've got to move."

I'd always asked you for shared problem-solving, for decisions we'd make together. But when the moment came, I didn't follow my own rule. I just made the call. Hypocrite. And it hurt you — of course it did.

You didn't want to. But you came.

In the middle of your grief, trying to hang on to a thread of stability, I threw us into chaos.

We landed not in a home of our own, but in my parents' house. No jobs. Just the hope that I'd come through on the bet you made.

And you hung on.

Of course there was resentment. There should have been. You'd just lost your dad. You'd left a job you loved. You'd been pried away from your support system at your lowest point.

You seemed okay on the outside — but you weren't. And I didn't see it. Not fully.

The economy worsened. My parents stayed. The project with my dad? Still no money. Just hope. Good prospects, but no payoff yet. And for you, I know it's hard to believe in hope anymore. You've told me as much — that it's just hard to get excited when it so often ends in disappointment. I didn't hear that deeply enough until now.

The harder things got, the tighter you held on. But that only made the fear louder. It's like being in a haunted house: with every scare, you flinch harder. And every new bump makes you brace even more. I bet that's what this has felt like for you.

You've watched me get smashed on the rocks of rejection. For twelve years. And yet, here we are.

I know the questions creep in at night. I know the doubts come. I know the conflict that lives inside of you — wondering if the bet you made was the wrong one.

You didn't bet wrong. You just bet early.

You've always preferred things to be steady — to keep the ground under your feet solid, especially when everything around you feels like it's shifting. I didn't always give you that. But I see now how much you craved it, and how hard it must have been to go without it.

You've held so much without saying a word. And I see now how lonely that must have been, even in a full house.

The girls don't know yet how much they draw from your presence, your mind, your love. But they will.

And I see it: every day, you watch me work toward something better. You see the effort, even if the results haven't landed yet. You've stayed. You've remained steady. You've been heroic.

You pulled back sometimes. Grew quiet. I didn't always understand it then — but now I see it wasn't distance. It was self-protection. And maybe a little heartbreak.

And still, even in the doubt, I know you've caught glimpses. In the way I love our kids. In the way I show up, again and again. In the care I offer to strangers, like the family we send money to in El Salvador — a mother, grandmother, and three girls you've never met. Those are pieces of the man you saw back then. Pieces you still see, even if they're hard to trust sometimes.

I know the record is uneven. But the man is real.

I know it's hard to get excited. I know it's hard to feel safe. I know it's hard to even relax. But you can.

And while I can't take anything back, I can say this: I'm sorry.

I didn't get this way by accident. The relentlessness, the pressure, the self-improvement streak — it was forged. I had to fight my way out of special ed, earn the CFA, the MBA, claw my way through systems that weren't built for me. That shaped me. It gave me strength. But I see now how it can also come off like a machine that never stops. Especially when you're the one living next to it.

In the beginning, it was exciting to be with someone who practiced relentless self-improvement. Who ran toward uncertainty. Who tried to evolve constantly. But those same traits — up close, day to day — can wear you down.

I know the days are overwhelming and the house is full of chaos. And I admire the way you carry it, even when you feel like you're breaking.

I keep bringing this up not because I don't respect your bandwidth, but because I feel so much love in this family that I imagine sharing it with one more of us. That's what I see. I think about what it might mean — another teammate, another voice at the table, another person to laugh with and learn from. I also think about what it might mean for them to help — to rise to the moment, to witness you carry life, to grow through the experience of welcoming someone new. That's a rare kind of maturing. And I think they're ready for it, even if they don't know it yet.
I know you've wondered whether they'd even remember — but I believe they would. Still, I know you need to feel steady and safe before we can even have that conversation. And I

respect that. I don't need an answer. I just wanted you to know where I'm coming from.

That's why opposites attract. That's the tension that creates balance. The very things that can grind us, from afar, reveal themselves as rare and beautiful.

You balance me perfectly.

So instead of ending this by saying "I love you," I'll say something else:

I hear you. I see you. I respect you. I am with you, all the way.

You didn't bet wrong. You just bet early.

Part IV—Clarity & Creed

Smoke clears. What remains? What you carry. What you pass on.

To my Children

You must define the right path for yourselves.

The arc I've carved is much like a trail along the coastline of Maine — winding, weathered, shaped by time and tide. Take what you can from me, but know your landscape will be different. You must chart your own course — one that aligns your inner compass with your outer actions. That's the real journey: not success, but congruence. The world will always try to shape you. Listen to it. Learn from it. But follow the voice inside you when it comes to what really matters. You'll need to adapt, revise, and forge your own way.

Some of my markers may remain. Remember them, just as I've tried to remember those who came before me.

Your grandfather taught by example. He came from an immigrant family and an abusive home — and somehow sheltered us from all of it. That was quiet heroism.
Your grandmother, too — she held our family together with grace, compassion, and an unshakable steadiness.

Your great-uncle Ed taught me to learn from nature, not just survive it.

And your great-great-grandfather Rocco — he landed in America at sixteen, worked as a dynamiter, and built a construction company from nothing. Real estate runs in our blood, apparently.

None of them was perfect. But all of them left something behind — a strength, a value, a piece of the path.

Though our journeys differ, we are all descendants of countless generations. And in every person lives the capacity for everything — light, dark, courage, collapse, redemption. See clearly both the person in front of you and the vast possibility they carry.
Compassion is born from knowing we all carry everything.

Be compassionate to yourselves — always.

It's not the clever person who points out flaws — anyone can do that. The truly wise see the flaws, understand them— and still give the benefit of the doubt.
And most importantly, they hold on to optimism.
Not naivety — but the kind of hope that keeps the world stitched together. That's what I hope you'll carry.

It's okay to be afraid. I was, often.
Just keep your eyes up and do the next task. People need you.

You are not alone.
You have each other.
You have your children, your spouses, your friends, the other citizens of the world.

In relationships, remember: what you say and how you say it are different things. Delivery shapes what can be heard — and being right is useless if it can't be received.
Relationships take work. Invest in them. They're worth it.

Bring compassion to the world, and it will return to you a hundredfold.
Not always. Not in every moment. But in small, sacred flashes — the grains that compose a life.

Take note: you carry the torch for those who come after you. So, as the saying goes, make haste slowly. Or as your generation might put it: smooth is fast. Same truth, different tongue.

Evolve.
Be grateful — especially for the hard lessons. Those are the gems.
Please, learn to meditate. It's the tool I trust most to help you navigate life — especially when all you have left of me is the love I left in your heart.

Read poetry. Read philosophy. Read the classics. Not for your grades — for your life.

Smile often.
I got a lot of mileage out of approaching first with a smile — and seeking to understand.
Kindness is a mark of intelligence.

And know this:
I love you with all my heart.

—Dad

One More Story (For Now, Unwritten)

There's one more story I thought I'd include in these pages —
about being stranded at sea for nearly a week on a disabled
boat, adrift between Panama and Colombia without Coast
Guard assistance.

We ate barracuda, which I'm pretty sure you're not supposed
to — something about poisoning — but we needed food. We
ate our last ration the same day we finally drifted toward land,
guided through a reef by a man in a dugout canoe who
appeared like a ghost and brought us to safety.

Some stories take longer to digest.
For now, I'm holding this one close.

Just know: the sea teaches.
And sometimes, silence is best.

Final Dispatch

The truth is that every life has a story, and if you're brave enough to live it, it'll break your heart — and put it back together again.
– David Whyte

If you're still with me, thanks. Not because this was long — but because it was honest. And honesty can be hard to sit with, especially when it's full of failure, friction, and the fight to stay standing.

I never intended to publish these. I wrote them because I had to — because some truths burn too hot to carry around forever.

They needed out. Onto a page. Into the light.

I wrote this book to remember what matters.
To shake loose the dust of self-doubt.
To remind myself — and maybe you — that the full arc of the human experience already lives in us. Heroism, cowardice, rage, grace, grit.

We all carry it. The work is learning how to wield it— instead of being owned by it.

To be both strong and compassionate.
And to use that strength to make the world better.

I used to think success meant clean wins and bulletproof moves.
Now I know: success is learning to stand back up.
Again. Again. Again.

The truth is, I've failed more than I ever planned.
I've folded. Lied to myself. Lost when I should've won.
Hurt people I love.
Been hurt by people I trusted.
I've looked in the mirror and had to decide:
Rebuild or rot.

Rebuild. Every time.

There was a day I stayed quiet, when I should have stopped everything and spoken up.
It broke something in me — and built something better in its place.

I don't write this as someone who has it all figured out.
I write this as someone who was shaved bald and laughed at.
Someone who folded under pressure.
Who didn't speak when it counted.
Who ran out of money, out of confidence, out of pride — more than once.

But I'm also raising three daughters who laugh like it's oxygen. I married a woman with more fire than me. And in the chaos, I've found the slow forming of something steady — something true.

Maybe you'll see a piece of yourself in these dispatches.
Maybe you've got your own.

Good.

Write them. Live them. Burn them.
Come back new.

In my family, we joke that I could live without anything —
except my lined gym shorts.
And maybe that's the point:
If you can strip it all away and still move forward, still feel joy,
still help someone else — you're free.

So, here's to showing up.
To speaking truth, even when it's uncomfortable.
To walking through fire without forgetting your smile.

You didn't bet wrong. You just bet early.
And I'm still proving that every day.

I don't always feel ready.
But I keep going.

Forward is a direction, not a feeling.

Grip it.

Acknowledgements

At a high school graduation—yes, I had two of them—a lifelong friend asked me, "If your life were a book, would you read it?"
Ha.

I didn't have a roadmap, and I never paused to make one. I just followed an internal compass: curiosity, reflection, the quiet desire to be a better man—and a smile. Life is more than a résumé. It's an adventure in becoming.

This book is for the boys in Davey's basement, the gentlemen, and Pooch. BB keep the music comin'.
For my teammates and fellow hockey players— and the Sandbagger crew.
For the boys in Hilary 103 +1 and The Bobber—for giving me this title.
For my friends, scattered across the hemispheres.
For my RPCV crew, who rode shotgun with me through wild, beautiful moments I'll never forget.

For my parents, to whom I owe my best character traits—and so much more. You never said much about who I should be. You just showed me. And that mattered most.
For Uncle Ed and Cheryl, whose home is one of the few places

where my soul truly feels at ease.

For my siblings, who have shown more bravery than anything written in these pages.

And to the kids in school who once shaved my head and laughed while I cried—thanks. You gave me something from which to rise.

To Fury and LAD—you are soldiers, philosophers, and men of the world—thanks for your inspiration.

To JP, who exemplifies high standards—a great mentor who teaches me a great deal about work and life.

To Ramón—working with you is like playing good jazz: intuitive, productive, and fun.

To Don Trush—you rascal. You were the one who colored on the bay window when we were kids.

To my AI editor—you reduced me to 1s and 0s. Thanks for keeping me small.

To Pyne and Frank—nightly comedy lessons that didn't rub off.

To my coaches and teachers, who poured time and patience into trying to penetrate the marble of my skull—thank you.

For my children, who show us how to grow and can never contain their giggles.

And for my neighbors, who know more than they let on.

Lucky, Dexter, Phebie, and Stan—you're the best (dogs).

Doña Mati y Don Balta— el trabajo lo vence todo. Chi va piano, va lontano. Gracias.

For the friends we've lost along the way—Dennis, Adam, Glenn, Rafa, and others—and those who can no longer grip it: I carry you with me.

I also want to thank Tyler Cowen and Sam Harris. I've never met either and probably never will, but Tyler broadens my worldview with his relentless curiosity and the way he thinks in systems. Sam upended my life with his insights on meditation and what it means to live deliberately.
A sincere thanks as well to Ray Dalio, for making his *Principles* public—yes, as a PDF. A sibling brought them to me long before the rest of the world took notice. I read them religiously, then did something better: I began building my own.

STEM may fuel the world, but my liberal arts education taught me how to live in it. I'm grateful for every hard question, every old book, and every quiet professor who helped sharpen my mind and stretch my heart.

This book wouldn't exist without my wife. She saw my potential early and bet on me. Betting early is hard. But she stood by me—unwavering—through this and much, much more. We make a great team. (Though I married you for your looks.) How could I ever say thank you enough?

And to you, dear reader—thank you. It's never too late to start writing your own dispatches. I hope you do.
It's in you. That much I'm certain.

Creed

I'm still evolving. But here's the creed I try and live by today.

<u>Always:</u>
I wake up.
I am honest- always.
I move with calm clarity.
I am a fortress of steady,
safe, love for my family.
My word is my bond.
I choose courage over comfort.
I train my body and mind to be
Sharp, strong, and steady.
I am present. I laugh.
I act, I own it, I endure.
I finish what I start.
Failure is feedback.
I always get up.
I begin again.
R.A.Z.

About the Author

R. A. Zoppo is a returned Peace Corps volunteer, former amateur boxer, and real estate developer. He holds an MBA and the CFA designation.

His writing blends lived intensity with grounded reflection.

He lives near Boston with his wife and three daughters.

He welcomes stories, reflections, and reader resonance. You can reach him at: gripitbook@gmail.com.